IN CONSTANT INCANDESCENCE

IN CONSTANT
INCANDESCENCE

POEMS
February 10 – August 13, 2010

Daniel Abdal-Hayy Moore

The Ecstatic Exchange
2011
Philadelphia

In Constant Incandescence
Copyright © 2011 Daniel Abdal-Hayy Moore
All rights reserved.
Printed in the United States of America

For quotes any longer than those for critical articles and reviews,
contact:
The Ecstatic Exchange,
6470 Morris Park Road, Philadelphia, PA 19151-2403
email: abdalhayy@danielmoorepoetry.com

First Edition
ISBN: 978-0-578-07608-9 (paper)
Published by *The Ecstatic Exchange*,
6470 Morris Park Road, Philadelphia, PA 19151-2403

Also available from The Ecstatic Exchange:
Knocking from Inside, poems by Tiel Aisha Ansari

Cover collage by the author
Book design originally by Ian Whiteman
Back cover photograph by Peter Sanders

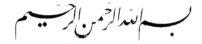

DEDICATION

To
Shaykh ibn al-Habib
(and the continuation of the Habibiyya)
Shaykh Bawa Muhaiyuddeen,
all shuyukh of instruction and ma'arifa
(and in memory of Shaykh Mansur Escudero)
and to
Baji Tayyaba Khanum
of the unsounded depths

––––––––

The earth is not bereft
of Light

CONTENTS

AUTHOR'S FOREWORD

I'm awaiting the arrival in the mail of a book by the great Muslim Sufi Saint, Abdal-Qadir al-Jilani, an excerpt of which I read on the internet, where he emphasizes the need to forget all about acceptance by humankind or advancement in the world, but to do all things always and only for Allah. I anticipate its healing power and its corrective advice, that as if I were a cork I would fit into a bottle, a wave and I would fold back into the sea among all the other waves, a patch of sky and I would patiently let clouds, sunbeams and hurricanes fill me and pass through me. And as I am, I would write these poems from my cradle to my grave (though I don't recall cradle poems and have yet to write deathbed ones, hoping I'm still able when the time comes) only for Allah, His good pleasure, and my unstinting devotion to His Merciful Beneficence.

I've witnessed firsthand many advanced beings who have done all things with this intention and reached this Gnostic knowledge, without presumptuousness nor pride, and seen the light they shed. So I know it is not only possible, but in-this-world achievable. And among flesh and blood persons, whose flaws may be subsumed in the cyclotronic shafts that maintain their spirits upward. Oh, I don't know... But having set out for some time now to open myself to poetic composition that hopefully goes to the roots of poetry rather than present-day worldly careers with their failures and successes, this reminder is what bolsters me to act in accordance with what may be a given as "higher stakes," going for the gold ring that is not worn in this world, and happy with my hand bare of such a ring until then, *Deo volente.*

I wonder why we do anything at all sometimes — I mean I sometimes wonder why we do *anything* at all. The field of actions is wide open, and being born with our mortal energies, we are compelled to act daily and nightly at some task or other, for good or for ill, desire impelling us. And why, with this giant twelve-lane avenue, some folk choose to act for ill is of course one of our eternal human conundrums, although as believers we must assume that the Divine Will, being behind and within everything that moves and has being and life, has a reason for letting evil occur. The great East Indian saint, Sri Ramakrishna, when asked why there was evil in the world, answered simply, "To thicken the plot."

But we are in an ocean of actions not only our own outwardly and those inwardly hidden within us, but actions everywhere swirling in constant eddies around us. We either drown in this ocean, or as some might, hold onto a splinter for floatability, or rise up out of it altogether, wetted through and through in our humanity, but as well, dry as a bone by our being held by divinity, acknowledged or not, like water off a duck's back, as they say, free of the deeper currents of this world's downward pull. Poe's *Maelstrom*. Lost in our little boat, going round and round as in the downward spiral of a drain.

How, then, do we "do everything for Allah," and keep our flexibility, our fluidity, our flightability, even our sanity? Do we remember, like the tick of a wall clock, to go back to our roots with each breath and heartbeat to remain free of those influences that either praise or blame us, lift or drown us, and instead bob happily on the surface and continue to the destined end hoping for eternity's vindication? Hearthrob tick-tock remembrance of our origin and goal, the *"divinity that shapes our ends,"* beyond this world's magnetic lusters?

As for poetry, *"I think continually"* of William Blake, furiously placid in his conviction that he's working for eternity through his voluminous productions of time. He too would get cantankerous about it now and then, though, and sad. But what a shine to his efforts, holding to his course without the Van Goghish vagaries that could drive a man insane. And after about the age of thirty, I transferred my hero-worshipping artistic allegiance away from Rimbaud, whose youthful work stopped abruptly while still in his early twenties, or Poor Vincent who drove himself, lion-like, to the brink and leapt into his own abyss, to William Blake who continued his work right onto his deathbed, painting gorgeous visionary illustrations to *The Commedia* of Dante, and singing of the blazing and angel-hearkening glories he already saw in his visionary eyes of where he was going. And this before I came across the aged (ancient and modern) Sufi poets whose "art," as radically florid and even surreal as any of my earlier favorites, is really triggered by their stations of remembrance of Allah, and based on experienced spiritual truths.

So, *In Constant Incandescence*, a play on words, light both *inconstant* and *constant*, is the work before you. You may judge its merits, and I am pleased if they please, but their words will lie between closed pages until they reach the hearts of readers who may also be corks, waves and patches of sky in their own right, and it is to you I direct them, and with this reflection that I present them to you. For Allah's sake.

Margaret dared to look at it, hearing its voice quiet and full of love, and saw that angels' faces are subtler machines than human ones. There were parts that worked sideways as well as up and down. It registered the finest changes, momentary and delicate, as it moved, like the iridescence on a pigeon's neck.
— Adam Foulds, *"The Quickening Maze"*

THE DISTINGUISHED AND ELEGANT WORLD

The distinguished and elegant world
from which all good comes

behind its clouds of genial obfuscation
and its furniture of assumed material existence

announces on various high-pitched trumpet notes
a general flowing into this world of

that world's spirit
attended by the highest manifestation of consciousness possible

much like silver orbs dangling in a turquoise sky
into whose midst from time to time

a flash of red fire exposes its
bright orange tongues to verbalize

what can barely be spoken by human utterance
so that an interpreter must be sent

who speaks our language into whose
poor vocabulary suddenly brighter words can pour

taking us out of our self-imposed exile
from our own best natures

and placing us with all certainty
into the pure saintliness of our original humanity

Suns and moons constellate our
mirror-like surfaces

Mountain peaks and deep lakes
landscape our plenitudes

in which no sparkling speck of cosmic dust
is left out

enabling us all to recognize
God's Light as its slants from His

remotest private chambers
into our hearts

2/10

THE FIRST ONE SENT

The first one sent was
great good Adam and his consort

great good Eve they both had wisdom
but willfulness overcame submission

though they spoke enlightened
words to their people

they could not resist wanting the divine
essence of God's knowing and its glory

for themselves which made them
naked whereas before their perfect

bare bodies gleamed in Paradise Light
unselfconscious since till then they

had no self apart from giant
flowering tree and rushing crystal stream

antlered deer and wheeling hawk

and all radiant and radiating
forms within and around them

whose names they'd heard them
repeat from themselves by God and

so repeated back to them in
high angelic company as well as

in the presence of the Envious One
who vowed to ruin them and

all their generations in time and
out of time on earth and

heaven
forever

2/10

WRITE ME A LETTER TO MYSELF

"Write me a letter to myself"
said a blank sheet of paper to a

pen *"that empties out the universe*
and replaces it with elements of light in

sweet constant motion some rotating around
a central axis some random-seeming in

leaps and bounds all held by the
magnetic will of God's ceaseless Living

Action in the world down to the finest
detail salmon fighting upstream larks

careening through trees in a riot of melodious song
only in this instance the light of

life within life the secret heartbeat
deep within the heart's deepest

secret place"

and the pen began to write what was
just written and the sheet of paper

atmosphere-thin so light shone through it
sailed everywhere where anyone took

a remembering breath in
saintly plenitude

and then through that same atmosphere
slipped out

2/11

EACH NAME GOD NAMED

Each name God named became a
four-legged creature or a two-legged or

no-legged creature wriggling along or
flying or floating on its own ray of

song from His own language to us
unknown but gave

Adam ears to hear it who then intoned
their given names and named them

in the angelic swirl of it seen and
unseen and also named the angels repeated to

him by them for he saw with sight
God-given to him

to see and hear God's each specific radiance
in full

plenitudinous obeisance

2/11

SOME DAWNS COME UP

Some dawns come up in a dark sky
some suns set in a sky of light

We take a breath and our
time has come

to take another

The earth slides out of its
own shadow

It enters a space in space
that's been held in place for it

then stays there long enough
to vacate it

humming to itself as it revolves away

The Merciful has made us
unaware we're hurtling through space

or even whirling on our own axis
whizzing in slow motion

past the stars

Having started out in the sky
we have to remain here

handing off wintry ice-balls and
dropping them through space

in this inviolable place

2/16

NEVER ENDING ARGUMENT

It's controversial and worthy of
never ending argument

God wears a bow tie and tends
divine bar in heaven

God leans down from a cloud and from
time to time points with His

forefinger

God is perpendicular to all that is
horizontal

God rides such a fast chopper we
can't see Him streak by

God's a long-bearded farmer in
Upper State running a wingéd horse farm

God spoke to a chosen few and from then on
has kept mostly silent

God's a giant eyeball in
space somewhere who sees us even

electron-microscopically

I'm even running into trouble with Him

right now writing all these

patently absurd examples

An absence Who's a Presence
a Presence Who's an absence

A something Who's never a nothing
A no thing Who's really something

Giant Technicolor alligator snapping its jaws
Solar eclipse that burns us all down

to a crisp

The list could be endless of all the
pins we set up at the

end of the lane to knock down

A smoky yellow-eyed panther lurking behind the
illusion of matter

A Friend a Foe
A smiling porpoise

A bridge to Nowhere
Nowhere itself

Sitting here with my mind finally
drawing a blank

I sit imperfectly still
I could be inside a tunnel at the

break of day

All whiteness can't exhaust the
inexhaustible whiteness I feel

Sitting up straight with my
eyes closed

I hear my dead parents
calling across the hedge

All the dead pets I thought were
mine wag tails softly purr cheep and stare with those

unlidded eyes of gold fish

Forgive us Indescribable One and
continue to put our

huge tasks before us

The day's never done without our
sweet service unfinished

extending beyond its darkness

2/17

WE ALL GO INTO OUR OWN MONK'S CELL

We all go into our own monk's cell at night
to dream our own dreams

The hardened criminal as well as the
eight-year old ballerina dreaming of

blue ponies

The murderous tyrant as well as the
genial old sea salt dreaming he's on the

deck of a trawler
dreaming mermaids

Each of us retreats into high asceticism
facing a wall of shadows and

bright colored cinema which present us with
both intractable puzzles as well as

sudden solutions

from that one world of dreams with its
six billion portholes at any one time

Shall the sphinx get up on its haunches and
stride across blue sands?

Oceans open up to their sugary undersea palaces?

Will the bloated corporate magnate fall down an
elevator shaft among a vertical flight of

owls reciting Buddhist sutras?

A sun-drenched field opens up and
field hands are coming home for lunch

singing glorious field-hand songs
and it's a gorgeous new world and we're

saved!

We struggle out of octopusial darkness of
agony and near defeat or from an

overlit operating theater where all our
organs have been exchanged for marsupials

into the light of day
like trembling creatures from a

long winter's hibernation

God having projected His pictures against our
soul's screen down to the

tiniest baby on earth who just saw
angels' wings scintillating up light-shafts in his sleep

and woke to this world
still fluttering with joy

2/18

IF I CAN IMAGINE A CIRCUS

If I can imagine a circus where
a hundred white tigers leap down in a

dazzling sleek waterfall of uninterrupted whiteness
pouring into a central spotlight

and a transparent balloon greater than the night itself
that rises higher than all our mental expectations

shimmering with unbefore-seen starlight

and that this universe with its billions of
gorgeously different galaxies some like

neon spiders in space some like oracular rainbows
is contained in a drop of air under a

divine microscope no bigger than the
dot over the "i" in the word "bigger"

Or that light itself is made from the
shimmer words make out of the

mouths of angels in dense rows and
complex geometrical latticework through space

or that the sound they might make if our
ears were wired to hear them were the

geologic deep crackings and explosions and millennially
eerie silences between the creation of

rocks and deeper down the actual crushing of diamonds

Or that all the trees we see are the
beard stubble of a sleeping giant held in the

arms of a cradling giantess ocean murmuring a

continuous lullaby of whales' low-decibel singing and
sleek sharks baring their teeth —

If all this can be imagined and far more than
I'm capable of this moment Philadelphia

4:10 a.m. with the lovely orchestral
quiet of multidimensional night pouring in my ears

and I can imagine God's vast audience hall
grander than any visualization possible

streaming through space whose majestic echoes themselves make
all colors and intermingled sound possible

as well as make possible the all of everything that
is in its emergence and disappearance —

because while we are simply dust motes in the light in this
hall afloat in His greater purposes

each of us is also a true imagination made
narrative in all divine dimensions whose

origin is Allah and whose end is Allah
whether or not we recognize it in this

life and lay down our lives for Him in
gratitude and servitude for it every moment

hearing His call past all imaginings to the
actual secret zero of our hearts

whose every beat is its visceral realization
past everything we can know or have

ever known
until now

2/24

A PARABLE WALKED UP

1

A Parable walked up to a low wall and
looked out over the fields and woods and

by his looking suddenly a strong golden
sun shone out through blue clouds onto

evenly spaced olive trees and running orchards with
irrigation channels runneling over which

flocks of starlings flew

He blinked his eyes and everything came to its
term and blossomed or fruited or started

building nests in the gnarly branches as the
blue clouds formed suggestive

shapes in the white sky

A Moral strode into a room with
heavy draperies and overstuffed

chairs and everyone grew silent while the
import of it hung in the air like significant smoke

somehow inspiring the various momentary inhabitants of the
chairs to sit straighter and see their

failings flash before their eyes to a
distant sound of a piano at which a

very poor student is practicing scales

Then out of the blue a Naked Truth strode
majestically along the beach by the

froth of silvery breakers
resplendent in its shininess and forward stride

and all the onlookers entered a new stillness in
themselves and cast off their doubts and

hesitations and behind the Naked Truth splintered off
shadowier but dazzling replicas of itself

all continuing to walk forward and look neither too
intently toward the sea nor too

intently toward the low mountains that were
off in the distance bursting into flame

No one moved
though sparks from the Naked Truth

mingled in every direction and entered whomever would
shiveringly make room inside them

A Poem sat down at an outdoor café and ordered
a very strong drink into which seemingly

a glitter of gold coins fell from nowhere
each with an engraved likeness of no one in particular but

each minted from God's own perfect manufacturing
each reflecting that first golden sun

breaking through those bright blue clouds of the
first stanza overhead

2

If the sun and moon should doubt
They'd immediately go out
— William Blake

Doubt fell upon its sword
and bled the whole world out

and not a drop of Doubt was left to
poison us further

We opened our eyes without their
usual film fuzzing the

light of everything and
everything's angels

spoke with one accord

Forests opened onto galloping horses
Heavens opened onto

drawing rooms of the most
congenial congregations

and hearty song was the *lingua franca*

to which the rest of creation could join
even to the stones on the ground

Water is purification's ambassador
to the flow that never ends

taking us from ocean to ocean

Our one true home surrounds us

3/1

SNOW SHOWER

A mind like a snow shower
unlimited dazzle

almost motionless
seemingly suspended

filling the whole sky
enjeweling the earth

all beauty resulting
everything unified

under a diamond blanket
sky and earth a single sheet

Step up we're in Paradise
step down we're in death's

ermine chambers
in absolute stillness

Door in the heart
through which all colors

stream
casting up perfect pictures

onto the mind screen
eyes like ancient ministers

open on the inside
xylophones under water

The snow sheet slowly
shakes imperceptibly

causing to gleam
the surrounding shadow show

God up ahead
God behind

all around us
nowhere to be seen

Saying this I blush
His Voice alone Supreme

My pen lifted
the writing goes on

White sheet of paper
white as snow

falling
ceaselessly

sky to earth
earth to sky

round again

3/6

EVERYONE'S GOING SOMEWHERE

Everyone's going somewhere or
doing something

Water spurting from a fountain seems to
fall into a pool

Even tree sloths catch sight of
tasty leaves and gravitate toward them

Dust doesn't seem to have to do much yet
falls and accumulates

What if we didn't have to do
anything at all or go *anywhere?*

First thing out of the womb we
wake up and sleep

A dynamic shiver runs through our souls

As if on the backs of a herd of lizards from
antiquity we lunge forward with our

eyes alert to whatever comes our way

And the light of each encounter is a
flash from Paradise

filtered somewhat deceptively into

brick buildings and dusty streets

But zebras and giraffes could just as
easily walk down them as we do

Our little hands with their
articulate fingers reaching for fruits

But what if we just stayed still?

Would water run backwards and the
air crumble?

Would the waitress who comes to
take our order draw a pearl-handled pistol

and fire instead?

Would the bulls of Pamplona
(all *doing* something and *going* somewhere)

still trample us to death?

A galaxy tilts into view
happy to be itself

It turns out to be our very own

There's all that space and
all that twinkling

And the echo of God's Voice
with no end in sight

ripples in its wild waves

3/7
(train to Hartford)

BEAUTIFUL THINGS

Sunlight on water is a beautiful thing
rushing past trees is also a

beautiful thing

People asleep aslant on train seats
can also be beautiful

The horn tootled at crossings is
hauntingly beautiful

A face in repose or in
animated conversation is beautiful

Backs of brick buildings sliding by
not beautiful but washed in a

kind of derelict beauty

The rattle and squeak of the train
rocking slightly from side to side

comfortingly beautiful and
rhythmically satisfying

The sudden blow of wind on the windows
symphonically pleasant

The coming home to you after even a

short time away

beautiful!

3/10

THE ONLY REASON

The only reason we don't go
up in a puff of smoke

is God holding the sides of our
ocean with His two immaterial Hands

And the only reason the earth isn't
buckling and erupting under us all the

time is His calming it the way a
horse whisperer calms a nervous colt

And the only reason we don't hopelessly
give up all hope at the first misfortune however slight

is His invisible beckoning from the other
side of His screen backlit by the

inhospitable galaxy around us where He's
rather miraculously made us our home

the pounding and breaking of icebergs and
mountains due to terrific forces always

at work inside and outside us

The oceans almost snapping completely
out of their basins with each

heave and frothy push shoreward
The unutterably gorgeous fury of it all

nearly unleashed at every moment as our
languorous blood rounds the bend at the

height of us and circles back down
and each star however defunct for

however many millennia before its last gasp of
light reaches us is somewhat firmly

(in our firmament at least)

in place each night where it
should be

And our words continue to be clearly
isolated enough to be comprehensible rather than

just a long consonantal or singly
voweled growl and within each of our

words a lovely or awesome territory of
existence with its own colors and weathers

abides in the realm of meaning —
all due to His compassionate vigilance on our

behalf for if it were solely
up to us we'd have

capsized ourselves and this dirigible
planet long ago as it heads ever

heavenward through the
high beam and low beam starriest

depths of
black night

3/12

CAUGHT

Caught outside the brothel singing a
sacred song

the saint sat down among his
pet scorpions and dispensed the

day's wisdom

Passersby noticed invisible umbrellas
crowding each other in the sky to

shade him

Insects also made an attentive circle
around him

refraining for a moment from
cleaning themselves to listen

Even the nearby river hunched up
closer to shore to catch a liquid

phrase or two in the
twinkling sun

Who's looked into a saint's eyes
and seen the next world

and then looked back at this one

with a fresh perspective?

All the worlds make a fist
in the saint's fist

then roll out again in sweet peacefulness
when he opens his hand again

There's no backdrop to this poem for his
shadow to be cast upon

You can see it go
everywhere at once

Oh wait a minute!

There's a 1940s style gas station in the
distance and a dusty pickup truck getting

gassed up for a cross-country journey

But where will it go in all this
glaring dustiness?

And how did it get to where it
is right now?

If the caterpillar could see he'd notice
a sly smile playing on the saint's lips

A dragonfly lights on his shoulders and stops

whirring its wings

Fish plop at the surface of the river
then swim away

*The first poem in a hundred years that
can't be finished before I*

get up to do something else!

Hallelujah there's any light at all
resplendent on earth —

And everywhere else

3/17

SUGAR OCTAGON

In a giant sugar octagon
the wages of the world are

won and lost

Flash floods come right up to our collars
and drown our eyebrows

We see through water

In the distance a murky city lies
landscaped in seaweed

It's always there the great
discoveries are made

The immateriality of matter
How air travels and goes nowhere

The materiality of light and how it
surges through the limbic system

Soft and innocent animals and their
fastidious eating habits

The nocturnal romances of ants
The contemplative life of spiders

Clarity comes and goes

but impermanence lasts forever

One white horse puts us all to shame
and if it's on a green hill in sunshine

that about sums it up for us
once and for all

The leakage from one moment to the
next is a matter for the

mathematicians of miracles

Sturdy life takes the place of
fanciful wishes

but can't stand up to a blast of epiphany
in a high wind of glorious song

If there's any more of this poem to come
it'll have to take place elsewhere

Check under things and on top of things
for any further traces of it

The whinny of that horse outside the window
The sudden tenderness as a

loved one falls asleep or wakes up
and looks you right in the eyes

and smiles

somewhere there's where God sprinkles
His largesse in unstinting abundance

and we recognize it in a place
both pre-lingual and post-cognitive

as breath sails into us and
out again as if on a

delicate surfboard of
sagacious nothingness

3/20

MY LAST NIGHT ON EARTH

If this is my last night on earth
I'm confident the dome will turn to light

the faces of all the stars will bend forward
and unheard sounds will stream from the

mouths of everything

If this is among the countdown of my
last moments *(and it is)*

snails will show their true colors at last
and fly away at great speeds on

supersonic wings

The furniture will crowd around to look
as it dematerializes completely away

whispering atom by atom into
total invisibility

Sleeves will roll up of their own accord
for the work at hand

Stairways to be built at all the far
corners of the world for safe escape

If this is among my final utterances

for all these years *(and it is)*

I would call no peacocks to display for me
nor banners to be suspended by flying storks

nor the colors of running water to braid into
one entwined choir of divine fluidity

nor darkened alleyways in remote cities to be
suddenly filled with fireflies enough to

illumine the destitute to a warm bed
in a cozy room decorated by children

or wish to visit all the places of my life one
last time *(and each place we*

visit is our last)

but just turn this page to continue this
poem to its inconclusion among the

pattering raindrops outside my window tonight
whose typewriting fingers are

tapping out Mercy's messages to
everything on earth at once in their sweet

one-way passage
out of here

3/21

THE SPACE BETWEEN US

The space between us and
what is Eternal

as we are now in our majestic
momentariness

a breath away from it —
just *that* much space!

A supersonic freight train
going by (almost a blur

though we can count the cars)

A spark's life
spat from a fire

hovering incandescent in the dark —
just *that* much space!

A caterpillar's peculiar life
meandering into butterflyhood

transformed in a hammock
of its own making

The amount of space all around us
and what is Eternal

in this space we'll
soon be out of

out of space and time
transformed in a

hammock of our own making
(not made by us at all)

that tiny breath of space
through which right now a

giant freighter bound for the
Cape of Good Hope could pass

all its stacks smoking its
shrill whistle blowing

though in this moment itself right now
we could be catapulted there

in a wink of light in a
speck of darkness

flash forward
out of *here*

and into *there*
by just *that* much!

3/26

CHILDHOOD OF THE SAINT

for Noah Leon Sanders

The childhood of the saint probably seems to
pass by in a matter of minutes

and he or she find themselves turning
wine into water and

stopping runaway school buses

A baby looks out at the world through
slitted eyes

not sure if the new accommodations are
really suitable after all

They suffer being picked up and laid down
gift-wrapped and unwrapped over and over

and no doubt we form later opinions and
attitudes in our tiny brain ridges

from the see-saws of these earliest moments

Whereas saintly babies get right to work from
the moment they land on earth

soothing the mother's fears bringing the
young father to the sudden

brink of maturity

They seem to remember their kaleidoscopic
journey through and past all the

worlds in their shattering lightning bolt
highlights and celestial rainbow shadowings

and the wild character of their various
populations enough to fill coffee table photo books of

undersea anomalies as well as gorgeous
extraterrestrial beauties

They open their eyes onto the blurred
cinema of this world and get

right down to business

They'd talk if they could but are
patient at the deficiencies of their new equipment

though some *(like the infants Jesus and Muhammad)*
utter perfect sentences then keep their

council until speech seems more
age appropriate for a more

natural consensus

But right at the first

these saints look at us with their

big watery eyes and we're
transformed

Birds gather in trees outside the
nursery window in perfect

Walt Disney fashion since they're the
news carriers to the rest of the

animal kingdom that another
saint's been born among the

usual run of ordinary mortals

*(the fact being that birds are more
capable than humans to spread*

the news in its original righteous language)

and when the light's out in the baby's room
and the parents finally go off to sleep

the true spiritual conferences begin
with elders and saintly substitutes

come from all the corners of the globe
and ancient domes of the stars

to confer with the newest saintly arrival

who might seem peacefully asleep

but baby saints are busy charting out
the needs and emergencies of all earthly human commerce

and when the enrobed elders in their brilliant nimbuses
finally return to their dazzling domains

they remind the saint to cry out in the most
robust and baby-like manner

to awaken the parents again to their
basic human assumptions

Later in the whizzing childhood of these
blessèd beings

(sawdust in their hair dirt on their
knees their pigtails tangled)

they have a touch that can't be described
and a piercing glance that rights

wrongs and wages angelic war on
injustices in the tiniest of matters

and the roads ahead of them already
glisten with their light having

brought God's intimacy with them
into the splendid

quotidian brightness of their days

Food tastes better in their company
financial worries disappear

(God's bounty falls from the rafters)

Everyone's clothed in a new nakedness
warmed by an anciently glorious sun

3/27

MADE OF GLASS

"We might as well be made of glass
Our consciousness looks out through a

kind of all-encompassing window"

This came to me as my
head hit the pillow to sleep

turning to my left and shutting my
eyes into deep blackness

These eyes the very same ones God uses to
see me according to Meister Eckhart

and who would contradict him?

All-surrounding consciousness that may or
may not include the one-day

mayfly or historical eruption of Krakatoa
when ash fell for weeks afterwards

even many miles away

Can I hear boats on the world's horizons?
Does the music of starlight reach me?

If the whole cosmos were twisted into a
single ribbon or like a

cloth wrung dry —

Well I can't even contemplate such a thing
this late at night actually 2:30 in the

morning and heading like a slow
train toward dawn

4/2

THERE'S A LIQUID

There's a liquid
one drop of which will

keep you drunk for days

But it goes by so fast
you might miss it

I've seen the bottle it's kept in
dematerialize at the horizon

and become first clouds of
superlative whiteness

then pure sky of a
spectacular blue

There's an air once breathed
our rib cage expanded around it

that lightly touches far mountaintops
and makes even newborn does quiver

There's an anger that falls out from our
sides like fans as we walk into light's waterfall

to the point we no longer
recognize ourselves in its glass

which when heated red hot and blown around air
contains the sky in its spectacular blueness

clouds in their superlative whiteness
and the bottle materializing at the horizon

that contains the liquid
one drop of which

keeps you drunk for days

4/3

A BLIMP OR "DIRIGIBLE"

A blimp or "dirigible" could do it
float above the earth full of

happy inhabitants
enter a pink cloud and

come out a blue one say or
look into a giraffe's eyes and see what

loftiness is all about with their
glamorous eyelashes

Or follow heat from a flame as it
rises in invisible ribbons and ask it

if being so combustible was worth it
ultimate evaporation so dematerializing

No!

Enlightenment here and now in
this body and brain just as it is

earthbound and death-headed in all our
orientations like a drunk compass that wants to

visit all magnetic directions at once

Purposefulness as eager as ants on a mission

One-pointedness as direct as a
church spire or minaret

tilting at the sun

Detached as those termite wings
that snap off as they hit the ground to begin

new termitariums for intrepid
aardvarks to invade

And hearts that see with telescopic eyes
what goes on in planetary spheres equally with

what goes on in God's own Radiance
right now before our noses

4/8

IN SPITE OF MYSELF

God who is The Inwardly Hidden and
The Outwardly Manifest

It is not You Who are hidden then but
myself

So if I come out from behind myself
will I see You?

My own visibility hides You?
My physical gestures of invincibility

— this sense of never-dying?

On a round earth suddenly
all its inhabitants are ghosts

We blend in with clouds behind us

The sun shines through us

I raise my head to the sound of
pounding hooves

Neither horse nor zebra —
It's the sound of our blood

or it's the sound of the ocean
or the ocean *in* our blood

a few gulls wheeling overhead

Or does it take that dear Lord?
Is it all quite visible after all?

Nothing but You as far as the
eye can see

the ear can hear

Yet You are not of it
nor are we

I close my eyes my hand
supporting my left temple

A lovely roseate sizzle
fills my sight

A whisper can start an avalanche

A star dies but its light
continues through space for thousands of

years

I love You in
spite of myself

4/10

WHEAT IS PARTED

Wheat is parted by the thresher
hair is parted by the comb

both to tame and take
advantage of their growth

So are we parted from our Beloved
that One to Whom we cleave more

dearly than we cleave to our own
selves

to thresh and comb us?

Separation is the key to union
when our consciousness matures

and we see we're not the
door we open nor the

horse we ride as we may have
perceived in childhood

when sun and moon were as
close as our mother's cheeks

And union is the key to separation
when we see the God we worship's

universe cannot contain Him
all those roseate hot galaxies beyond

vision and fathomless space whose shape our
unenlightened eyes can't fathom

wider than all swirling shape and blackest light
beyond every conception even of

beyond

But our hearts can

4/14

BE KIND

Be kind to your shoes
it's not their fault your

feet hurt and miss slipping
into them the first time in the

dark

Be kind to the others at the
table who may be hungrier than

you though they may also be
observant of your needs

Be kind to soap that can only
last so long frothing off your

superficial grime

Be kind to sound that goes
everywhere at once and strikes ears

waiting for the call or simply
sensitive to noise

Be kind to the sun that
appears at our horizon as we

tilt toward it swinging

around it whistling as we

go

Essentially kindness is an elixir
that turns rock to gold hard

hearts to running streams

and is enshrined deeply engraved on
mystic tablets just inside

the shadow of the cave

Every creature shows kindness
when it's not afraid

Flakes falling through the air are kind

Ourselves falling
as we die

4/23

KEYHOLE

If you only have a keyhole to look through
polish it and make it shine

If your horse is three-legged
stand it by a sun-drenched mural and

feed it sugar

The moon has the knack of
shining for everyone

Lovers and murderers
thieves in the night and

saints at bedsides

Why would a waterspout in the
loveliest ornamental garden

only go so high before spraying its
drops down again in the surrounding pool?

If the light comes at a slant perhaps
we should stay at an angle to

catch its salubrious rays

If the wind messes your hair it's
really a new hairdo

And if the door remains closed against
Kafka and his ilk it's really no

matter we need to tend to though a
similar door may open for us at a

later date or remain as locked as it
was for poor Franz

I believe the Presence of God appears for
everyone and inspires imaginative ways to

avoid humiliation or slaughter

Though the glimpse of His Love may come
a split second before succumbing

in that instant all of Paradise in its
bedazzling full colors appears

A railroad crossing is a
good place to stop and

look both ways

Many a life has been lost in the light
as well as the darkness

How's your three-legged horse?
Are the pickles as tangy as last year?

The desert loves the lost wanderer so much
she takes him to her hot bosom

The sun loves bleached bones
the way a bride her diamond ring

Take heart in the instant of
losing it

God's platter has strange fruit sometimes
but the pips are always the same

If we head back the way we came
we're sure not to miss it

4/24

A LITTLE PEDDLER

A little peddler appeared by the
side of the road peddling

impossible outcomes and hopes beyond
hope

Although he appeared to us in this world
his wares were not quite of it

and that was the rub

People might buy and take them home
and find they'd only work in that

surrounding interpenetrating and
intersecting realm that is actually

not of this world at all though its
reflection might appear here and if

the new owner of these incandescent
items truly possessed them

things in this world would go
that much smoother or they'd be

blithely insouciant of the outcome anyway
come what may

with stars in their eyes in any case
whatever people might say

"Buy now pay now
Buy later pay now"

(there was never *"pay later"*)

He had a number of business plans he'd
take out of his tattered coat lining and

spread on the ground at our feet for
prospective buyers to ponder

He'd wink a little pull at his beard
chuckle in a totally disarming way

and only the darkest souls among us
would pass the offer by

Later they might run to the place where
he'd appeared *(following that rosy scent)*

but he'd be gone before they arrived

The happy buyers who'd taken
advantage of his offer might

give them some of theirs
(even theirs only on loan)

but dark souls would have to
blow with their own heart's breath on the

incandescence
for it to really shine

4/25

THE LOUSE THE LEACH THE ROACH AND THE HELICOPTER

The louse the leach the roach and the
helicopter all must have their day

But even the pyramids at Giza are now
nothing but stone and their

spirit paraphernalia moved on to
other realms

A golden bicycle atop a hill of light
Some far off galaxy imploding whose

debris won't be visible to us for another
hundred million years

The first smile of every child
The last grimace of every executed criminal

Earnest worker ants carried off in a flood
Tippy-top buildings built for bravado alone

Every way so craftily sculpted by
gravity and wind that grows to almost

tsunami size but the next moment's
flat as the Gobi

Any argument that comes between us

as suddenly and without warning as

that wave and that *tsunami*
heights of love and depths of despair

are only a fleeting expression on a
saint's face as he whistles down the lane

having seen the world firsthand and having
had its taste and its aftertaste

and whose eye blinks are an entire

sunset and sunrise as he goes
putting to rest all doubts about

the exact location of reality which is
neither inward nor outward but

both at once and simultaneously
neither

as the horizon rounds toward us on its
momentary circle under our feet

(and lucky our feet are rollers
or we'd fall over

and lucky our hearts have God in them
or we'd have fallen and rolled way farther over

long ago)

4/29

THE DRUNK IN ALLAH

The drunk in Allah are
free from the roll of the dice

The drunk in Allah swim in the
mercy of His love

The drunk in Allah take both
roads at the fork

*(and can do so because they're
drunk in Allah)*

The drunk in Allah eat caviar when they
eat dry biscuits

drink the best vintage wine when they
sip water

They're here hobnobbing with ants and
butterflies and converse at length with

the spider in her web

The drunk in Allah would never let on
they're drunk in Allah unless they're

drunk in Allah

They enter a hospital and come out

shaking like an invalid

enter an old people's home and come out
the death of all of them

enter an orchestra and come out the
whistle on a garbage barge heading into

gray waters

The drunk in Allah have
one thing in mind put there

by Allah

Having given up themselves they're
brought into sunlight like

washing set out to dry

They don't do anything on their
own anymore

If a bricklayer hired them the
wall would be done in a flash

or it might take a year
or never

Drunk in Allah

5/3

HEAVEN

Heaven is a crack in the ceiling of the
light above us

black night full of white clouds and moon
giants can't tumble down from

Heaven is sword-points shooting
from stars and showering the earth with

needle stings

Dew from heaven moistens our fingers and
cheeks our eyelids and others' eyelids

among us

We laugh in its fountains and
fall in love with its blades

eternally turning in strictest rotation
above us

A face bends down through its turns
to water our tears with us

to heal us

5/8

LINE FROM A DREAM

We hear robins too I think

over the golden road

5/10

THE PRESENT TENSE

You wake up and the room is empty
the light is out

There's that high-pitched ringing in your
ears or in the air of cosmos

Somewhere a crescent-shaped boat is
rocking back and forth on triangular waves

in pale moonlight

Somewhere a child is growing a new tooth
a salamander a new tail

Someone is making up a story to fascinate women
mislead the police or

write a book

Everything comes clean in the end
even the end

and the end is near
at both ends

which meet
under God's tablecloth

where the feast is being set out

in golden ewers on sparkling trays

fruits like you've never seen
sweetmeats of indescribable hue

shimmering as they transform into the
most gorgeous music and

back again

Come on there's still
time to catch it

Your life hasn't gotten
that far away from you

The room is empty
but your heart has a pillar of flame

from which a phoenix launches its
renewal in a fireworks of ashes

Worlds within worlds
in this empty room

in the present tense
that never slackens

5/11

ON THE TRAIN TO HARTFORD

On the train to Hartford
out the window in the rain

the apartments are full of people
and the people are full of pain

Or are they? Holding to little
mouse tracks each seeks

its happy way
some with little and some with

much to say
but as much as possible

holding pain at bay
with greater or lesser success

and a lot or a
little to pay

5/12

SHORT TREATISE ON DISTRACTING ONESELF FROM DISTRACTION

When angels fill your doorway
greet them with plates of

glistening cherries and purple
grapes they will not eat

A cloud or two overhead should
shield you from the sky's anger

Put before your face all the
faces in the world and light their

candles with a single flame

Let your heartbeats dictate the
height of your contemplation

the soul's longing dictate the depth of your
concentration

your body's utterly material reality
the evanescence of every passing thing

If you were sent to count the
zebras in Zambezi where would you

begin?

If the waves of the sea each had a
name where would you hold

roll call?

(Every wave has a proper name)

The actual dimension of the air
is as close to our senses as the

whinny of a horse

Once you begin to distract yourself from
distraction a space opens up

No plot of land should go unfenced
yet your inward vision of landscape

rolls freely over hills and cliffs
from sea to sea and sky to sky

A flake that lands on the
sand in front of you is yet another

mirror that predicts your
fall

Don't let smoke
camouflage the locomotive

If you interrupt someone at breakfast

nightfall may become calamitous

A certain springiness in your step
should remind you earth's

hurtling forward through space

We wake up in God's domain
tiny in His dimension

How dare we think otherwise about the
creation of island chains depths of

icebergs and the flashing of seasons?

Each star calls to another star
by its exploding light

In stillness pray
In commotion remember

Leaving everything out
is a way toward emptiness

Neither the flowing stream nor the
towering mountain are

adequate to the task

If you've come this far you must
continue to the end

And the end is both near and sweet
and just a beginning

The beginning has begun in mid-breath and
mid-sentence

The song we sing when we
lie down to die

is the same song we'll sing
on the other side

5/25

BECAUSE

Because the greenness of a valley
comes from the stars

and everything reflects the beauty of heaven

Because trees are rays of heaven
whose crowns are roots

clenching the earth

Because ocean waters
lap our shores longing to be

embraced by the continents and whomever
inhabits them

A silver bird is no greater than a
red bird or a brown bird

and when the sun goes down all the day birds
huddle together

Because the heart is a curious puzzle
whose cut edges fit together to form

the only known image of God
as it ripples without ripples across the

face of the waters

Because thundering herds that
reverberate the earth

can be felt up our legs when we
cross busy streets

Because the original people have
never left us

Their mark is in space the way
space occupies time

and when we listen closely we can
hear them humming to themselves

melodies our nonchalant hearts compose
in our nonchalant hours

Because all this and more
and the way light slides off a roof

into the First Garden

And once you've heard the singing of the
saints as they walk its paths

you won't listen to
anything less

And because pebbles and stones dance for
joy on the road when they pass

and even their passing shadows are worth as
much as a glimpse of them

from tip to toe
that we can never see

in their divine entirety

And because I'm lost in the wilderness
sometimes crying sometimes

keeping silent

not covering my eyes half enough
from the evils of the world

Because we're all trying as
hard as we can not to

fall into despond though if we're really
attentive everything and everyone needs our

undivided attention
until the end of time

This lifts off about here and
hovers slightly above ground

hoping some of its moisture
waters the young shoots below

but never so far above earth that
the rich soil of its intrinsic makeup

fails to filter up into the reality of its words

Because nothing is anything less than a
full reflection of God's Face

beckoning us
down the road

free of danger

Sweet Residence
of nothing

but His Name

this radiant sensation
that reverberates us

home

5/26

BREATH THAT IS EVERYTHING

The roar of engines
and the landings and the

takings off

The silence of night with its singing
bird insomniacs

The rush of time like blue silk
veils in the wind

or is time pale gold veils
with loose fringe?

He stands
the hero of this poem and briefly

salutes nothingness

Then sees his folly just before he
transforms into stone

at the edge of a stony abyss

and his apprehension multifoliates in
cylinders of green that

open as they whirr in
revolving ascendancies

And the flush world of whispering
correspondences pulsates throughout

the space left by his abandonment of
error that periscopes him to

vaster sunlight

Ripples of solar wind that
reach our shores

The oceans' unhesitant joy

Breath that is
everything

5/27

EVERYTHING PERFECT

Adam turned to his wife and found her
more beautiful than he could have imagined

standing in a half-lit grotto the sound of
waterfalls birds a click of snapping

branches sounds of growing stems of
flowers outleaving stretch of vines

reaching for tendril-holds sound of lion's
roar in the far mountains and

the *baaing* of sheep

She looked at him with fresh eyes
and found him compellingly beautiful also

looking at her and glowing the sky
darkening on their first night together

And so many generations coming after them
written lightly in the air around them in

breeze-wisp calligraphy the names of
each of us and everything else

Their faces were to each the highest reflection of
divine symmetry and sacred proportion as

anything in creation and everything in
creation seemed to swim in each other's

features or be indicated by the
fierce or gentle sweet or deep

light in their eyes

Their hands touched and
vines entwined them

uttering no words
but each action lexicon-filled to

bursting so palpably readable each
meaning to which a word or

cluster of words could be ascribed

and each silence pregnant with
deepmost silences

until we come to us
in identical dimensions

Adam with first gestures
Eve with first love

Everything perfect

5/31

THE WORLD IS TRULY A POPULOUS PLACE

The world is truly a populous place
and each of us has assigned above us

a triangular star that like a celestial
cookie-cutter slices through space a

channel for divine inspiration direct as
light but more intense and subtle so as to be

almost indistinguishable from the haphazard
accidents that seem to abound for us

at every turn and crossroad

We're not snails on a one-dimensional
road but travelers in tetrahedrons and

vehicular radiolarians of complex
directions and offshoots

always as if we're going somewhere on earth
but often standing perfectly still in the

vibrational sunshine of God's greater activity
so that if on a boat the mountain moves

and if on a mountain the boat moves
and inner channels of supreme animation

begun in the life womb in this world
enliven our stride

"The handle came off in my hand" you say or
"The door is irrevocably stuck"

but when you turn away a herd of
ostriches bounces happily through in their

balletically illimitable way having
called your bluff since that

door was always open all along
nor were the walls around it to

define its "doorness" really ever there

This may sound strange coming from a
glass pipe stuck up from the ground

but all our activities as we
wander this earth making either

sweet fools of ourselves or piles of money
or both

actually take place in heaven or in a
kind of heavy heaven that more resembles

earth but whose xylophonic resonance
is actually heavenly

as clusters of rainbows fly away in
flamingo formation

across the wide Saharas of our heartbeats

6/2

LET THE SHIPS ARRIVE

"Let the ships arrive
in all their gaudy splendor

and the cargos they contain
be taken on shore!"

I didn't hear this landlocked in
bed in Pennsylvania nowhere

near a port or salt-sea smell of
ships

Nor in this case dreamt that I
know of with what scraps I

might have been left with and this
phrase might well have been from

that
but the phrase came onto or into

me clearly upon my regaining
waking consciousness and who am

I to resist it or let it fade by when
there's the scant promise more might

come and a poem result?

Way in the deeps a Helen is
refusing to appear

My consciousness hears no Titanic nor
Pequod drawing near no

Ahab stamping on the upper deck

All's quiet in these waters

Let a similar peace reign
in a similar sea

and on a similar shore

6/5

SPEAKING ENIGMATICALLY OR STRAIGHTFORWARDLY

If we try to speak enigmatically
a blue owl might fly into view

spilling the beans in
simple declarative sentences

While if we try to speak straightforwardly
about subjects more abstruse say than

how plumbing works or what's gravity
suddenly armies of green spiders each with a

very long word taped to its back might
saunter spider-like onto the scene to

complexify if not outright mystify
our so well-intentioned meaning

A ball hurled high will nevertheless
have to fall to the ground *sometime*

and water poured on an inclined plane
has to keep flowing downward

and as for plumbing well that's also
not that easy to explain

But try me on God's mysterious ways or

why once created every mote and

mouse in the universe still needs His
direct supervision and I'll sing a

song or two off or on-key about just about
anything to convince us all including me

that although each living one of us
knows in the depths of our bones the

perfect answer still a certain shyness and
humility is called for and a

kind of fineness that leads to a
generous silence after all

aerial parades of blue owls or
green spiders searching for purchase

notwithstanding

6/8

IN THE LAND OF MAKE BELIEVE

In the Land of Make Believe in which
most of us live

a nail through a board can be
terrifying

and death in its cold body its hammock stretched between
two eternities can be

a blackout altogether until
white doves reconvene in their sweet

cooing halo over everything

Our horizon shall be only full of
exotic flowers in all the rainbow colors after a

rain in a gulch where pots of gold accumulate
and rings of gossamer dancers abound

Oh yeah

And the very sound of that nail going
through wood is a wrenching and a

wakeup call from being ourselves bored to
ourselves but being now the board the nail

penetrates with its pointed truthfulness

The all scattering world-shattering
shedding of fairy tale images to a

wall extending upward past the empyrean

a sobering if not outright death blow to
all we hold sacred yet in fact

the most sacred thing of all
as I experienced at the Kaba's wall which

did just that
the nail in this case my being

utterly alone with Allah

"deeper than did ever plummet sound"
all sound disappeared around me then

returning to find me still there
facing the black cloth with its

scattered white moths haphazardly
clinging to it

(in all their perfect locations)
forever buttoning my heavens

6/9

SEE THROUGH MATTER

See through matter
to the Name

through the Name
to the Named

and each time
before the Named

His Light
hit your dark

facets with His
Face

whose glance
dissolves

interference
to the Name

and through the Name
to the Named

6/15

THE LEAST BIRD SONG

It almost doesn't matter which way we go
we're going to confront it anyway

or what colossal corridors we take to
get there

or how many deserts we cross in bare feet
or how many banquets we attend in

ermines and pearls while the
blue waters below crash against black rocks

or what years are upon us or how few times we've
gotten lost in the tangly woods to be

found safe and sound by a search party or
solitary woodsman

or how many seas we've crossed in the
same boat with our foot jammed in the

hole in its hold to keep us from sinking

It almost doesn't matter looked at
cosmically from a star's point of view

The silhouettes are going to shoot up to
send us their symbolic messages

Some of the actors will leave the encounter while
new ones in more austere hats arrive with

fresh dialog and uncanny plot twists

The high wall before us will inevitably
show itself with those darling

white clouds hanging around up top

and the sleepy watchman will show us
one sly eye in recognition of our arrival

And yet how different the paths of the
bereft from those who sing as they go

and who let world's glow shine its
golden highlights on their eyelids and cheeks

whose energies are not kept in stoppered bottles in the
bottom drawer but animate the

constant gorgeous horses running along their hearts'
horizons against a perpetual sunset

and whose words weighted on the scales of love
always weigh down the pan rather than

land weightless in a
windowless shop with no cross draft

And for whom the least bird song at dawn
is cause for irrepressible joy

6/19

"EARTH HAS NOT ANYTHING TO SHOW MORE FAIR"

"Earth has not anything to show more fair"
can hardly be called natural speech

(*though I misremembered it as* "hath")
yet it conjures already peaceful imagery

or a kind of prelude to imagery like a
soft two-handed upper and lower register

piano chord rolling into a new phrase
and though no great fan of Wordsworth

(*I side with Blake*) yet when I
stilled my mind before Dawn Prayer this dawn

his magnificent line came to me unbidden

and framed by the first slat of it at least
this short and odd penetration into

how making beginnings leads us further in

and I see now instead of
"ships towers domes theaters and temples"

a single giant ship's hull darkening the sky
and bearing down on me

and hear a crew of crazed gypsy sailors
throwing curses around like angry ropes

and think of it carrying deep in its
clanking hull explosive contraband or

casks of filched pre-colonial jewels and
hammered masks of gold or encrusted emerald shields

slithering back from mercurial plunder

Deeper in the heart there are heavy doors it is
forbidden to enter without

golden birds on our shoulders
whose angelic nature slenders us for

the passage unmasking and unshielding ourselves

And if we enter we are instead ourselves the
emerald of our goal made manifest

held up in the sunlit shaft of our victorious insight

This incremental travel inward past our
self-imposed obstacles of transit

and certainly *earth* in all its transitive glories
has not anything to show more fair

than this!

7/2

HEADING SHOREWARD

Heading shoreward
will the gulls in their gray jackets

as they swivel their white heads from
side to side to survey the scene the

tides the tossed-aside scraps and our acrid and
sacred selves down below in our

puffed and brave puniness walking the beach
be angelic hosts?

Will salt waves hold aloft ghosts of
wrecks or their wretched crews

as we stride in blithe indifference to their
fates along the sands millennia later

as those tiny white crabs dart deeper into
wet shadows leaving only punctured breath-holes

on the surface?

As we skirt the continental edge in
broad daylight avoiding direct sunlight's radiant ravages

will earth's upheavals shade into shadow
or show human heart's shadowier side still

as we saunter by lips of surf
frothing such peacefully baby-like

bubbles light hits and glisters with
blinking crescents

before dissolving away?

7/5

GROWTH

Some of our growth takes place
in the womb of our mother

The rest of our growth takes place
in the womb of the world

7/6

IN CONSTANT INCANDESCENCE

1

A boy is meant to deliver a
huge wheel of gouda cheese on the

handlebars of his bicycle

He squints at the top of the
hill at the destination a few

hills over at the

stand of cypresses the ones where the
choir of angels always practices its

sustained high notes in the
leafage as he passes

*"Deliver it to Monsieur Descartes
and hurry back!"*

"Yes, sir" says the boy in the crisp
autumn air

He heads out

The day has taken its lozenge of beauty
which is just now taking effect so that

every light on things' edges has a
delicate golden cast and every

shadow delves into a deep brown darkness
of definite mahogany hue

"Adieu —To God!" says the cheese maker
"and then right back"

But he didn't know God's pre-mapped
subterfuge for the boy to grant him

eye-popping epiphanies starting today
and heart-rending teachings from the

very core of things to the very extremities of his
body and the branching articulations

of his mind

How could he know? He makes
cheeses all day

in huge vats with its various
crucially delicate processes just one of which

botched and the whole vat made useless

"Yes sir!" says the boy again halfway down the hill and
with his right index finger pulls at the

bicycle bell whose high sweet dulcet tones
ring out over valley and copse and

alert the angels who are
congregated in the cypresses of his

impending passage

2

Monsieur René Descartes constantly ponders
the existence of himself to

find out if he exists

and is often no nearer than Chuang Tzu's
dream of himself as a butterfly or as a

butterfly dreaming he is a man
such are the abiding ambiguities

even though the afternoon sun slants
its beam all the way from that

raging orb's surface like a blisteringly volcanic pomegranate
through his study's window right onto

his flat astonished face
both illuminating him momentarily and even

warming him slightly this lovely autumn afternoon

But no
it gives him no certainty even as his

atoms are combusting and breaking down and
recombining to make that very elusive

René Descartes return a wide-eyed
but shifty reflection in his glass

although as he constantly keeps thinking and therefore
takes that constant thinking as his constant

that will have to suffice for him to
establish his existence once and for all

as the gouda cheese makes its
wobbly way past copse after angel-filled

copse and especially the little lake where
God's Face always appears to the

boy on his bicycle and for a deep brief moment
shatters his sense of himself in a

million flying sparks of recognition
of that grandeur greater than he is

pumping at the pedals to gain
traction to go up the first hill to his

divine appointment

3

"Lord if You were less than You are
the mountains would crumble

And if You were more than You are
we'd never know You"

sing the cypress trees

"Yet everything is less than You Lord
and nothing equals You in greatness"

sing the lake waters

All we know is the singing in the trees
and the way the waters ripple into

glittering features

The coast is clear for
seeing and hearing

The sky cannot reach Him
yet the earth is His mirror

We come and go
and He remains

before us and after us
to which we tune in

But His absence is nothing
compared to our own

His Presence the tie that binds

SIPHON

If we could siphon all the light in the
universe into a single place

from ancient as well as future stars
or from the light in children's faces

running alongside trucks in the Hindu Kush
hoping for *baksheesh*

or the light that breaks over the lavender
iris-strewn valleys they live in

or the light in the excitement a physicist
sheds who's made a significant breakthrough

or a mallard's iridescent green head as it glides down
onto a lake

or inconceivable light that inevitably
escapes such puny enumerations —

would that concentrated illumination be
what resides in our human hearts?

We fade and glow into and out of it
though it centralizes ourselves and everything

with its incessant cyclotron
universally recognizable no matter

what language we speak
angelic or less so

pale blue ecstatic stutterings of chromium
flakes that scatter through everything

or poured steel-vat solar conflagrations of
burning orange hot enough to melt a tank

Spatterings from planet to planet in dark space
their own speech the speech that intertwines us across

light years and whose language we almost hear
when we bend our faces close to our

cats' faces and touch noses

that envelopes our hearts and
envelopes our houses on no matter

what dark hillside in whatever
metropolis or town

as well as whatever magnification from
microscopic colony wiggling under a

microscope to the very entirety in all its
deafeningly silent glory from

universe to universe

And that's the light we lean in close to our hearts
and hope radiates our faces as the

first face of our being and the only
imperishable one after all

God's Light in constant incandescence
Who says only the heart can

contain what He is in His indescribable essence
and from whose constantly illuminated

streams come all men and women both
outside and inside us as we ourselves

join the rivering flow that
unites us before our births and after our

lives have gone over this world's cascade's edge
into the glittering bright mist below

7/13

WHAT GETTING OLD'S LIKE

"If this is what getting old's like
bring me my zebras and snow leopards

and let loose my giraffes to
lope free across the plain" grouched the

old graybeard who just noticed creaks and
creases gronks and low honkings his

gracefully dilapidating body was
extending through having

started as a young man able to
bicycle with a cheese on the

handlebars to this anthology of sharp twinges
who has to hold to the wood

railing to pull himself upstairs

Not that actually aging was
unknown to his brushed up mind itself

nor the gold coin of death
sizzling down through the stacked bills of

paper money in their
neat rows

Nor the way windows fill with
crows who don't need to

speak to tell their tale but just
fly over graveyards and

dip their wings sunsetward

But squawking shanks ache along his shins
and simple bone wrenches as they lie

perfectly still write the page-by-page

dictionary of time passing and pains increasing and the
pages are fluttering by

may God bless them and *Oh!* gild their
edges with His

incandescence as they go

7/15

I CAN'T LIVE FOREVER WITH THIS BODY

I can't live forever with this
body and these organs with their

mish-mash jumble of perfectly
organized functions each fairly quietly

going about its functional business
squirting this chemical or expelling that

tiny splat of now depleted whatever into
perfectly receptive wherever as I

sit or stand or lie on my side either
awake or asleep grim or smiling smart or

as blank as a fence

We seem so united to our bodies and their
strange array of internal subway transport

going through dark bluish Tantric tunnels by a
faint and curious iridescence continually

carrying on with more earnestness and
sincerity even than we have from

moment to moment the
long suffering liver the *oompah-oompah*

heart with its martial regularity and
occasional faint lapses from the

heat perhaps or to just interject variety
and the brain *Oh my God* the brain

somewhere up here behind the eyes and
generally under our hair if we still

sport such luxurious strands

And then of course the eyes God's periscopes God's

keyholes God's envisionings by which we
see God's wonders everywhere direct

Oh how lovely and attached are we to these
orbs we open each morning first thing and

close as the last thing each night no
matter how many doves cross

turquoise purple skies or how many
whole red roses fall through white waterfalls into bliss

and our hearts seized by the beauty

At some point at any point by only
previous or instantaneous appointment

at the divinely scheduled moment of

itself by itself

this body will say farewell to the rest of me
and the rest of me will disenvelope and

disembody and pull away and go over
sailing where birds go and where

actual birds do not actually go but only our
bodiless ones in their new pure swimsuits of

Godly glory and supernatural latex
at one at last with the

element through which we swim
and even taking that element itself with us

as we swim there
uproariously singing

7/17

THESE ONE THING

Forget the alabaster urn the donkey cart
Ripcord laid along a wobbling porch

Rain tree in a country with no rain
Ice patch at the top of darkling flame

Forget the low moan emitted from
below the boards

Roan horse coming home from no display
Lengthening hair strand from Magnella's brushing

Perpendicular variance in the
quadrilinear pool

with no trace of anything from the
hand of man

Forget the loose draped cloths of this world
around our shoulders

The nothingness awaiting all this
grand commotion

The small whispering whimper one
afflicted makes

we can't forget no matter
how we try

Teardrop on a cheek a lover places there
from her heart

Forget the whole world for this teardrop
and her heart

Forget the whole world for these
one thing

God's echo
absorbing it

7/17

THESE ONES

The courageous ones
who get up to give their

seat to a caterpillar

The ones who stop a blizzard
with a smile and their

teeth freeze

The grandmother lost in the snow who
drops her needle and

finds true north

The child in a pumpkin carving from
inside the face of its

ultimate liberation

The single-minded ones against whom
the world like a flurry of newspapers

flattens its noise

Jumpers and leapers into an abyss
that becomes a linoleum floor

who do so to keep greater ones

from falling

The lion-hearted mouse person who
casts no shadow through

no fault of its own

The howl at the end of a hall
that comes from a heart

seized with glory

Allah's endless inspiration over all
and our acquiescence to

magnify His Grace

The fly that leaves a room willingly
and the angel whose wings

cover the house

7/17

DEEPEST PHOSPHORESCENCES

The natural repose of everything really
is rapture

Like coiled springs everything waits
to be sprung

In meadows in sunlight peace is a trampoline
and buds of tiniest flowers

when no one's looking
clap their petals for joy

On city streets with everyone's determined expressions
innermost flight *(sometimes downward)*

is palpable

Light itself as it swirls around us
flickers brighter then dimmer then

hurries itself into almost blinding
exuberance

Oceans barely contain themselves
throwing themselves onto beaches then

withdrawing to contemplate their deepest
phosphorescences

We can barely keep from leaping into the air
even as our stepladder bones think

otherwise and we have to wait for
sleep to take off into literal

atmospheres of transcendence

Animals are always on the lookout for an arc of
energy to ride on

as worms hunch forward happy in their
mud-bound gymnastics

while birds above-ground interweave darting and
swooping with those of the closer angels

God isn't static though we
can't glimpse Him passing by the

window

Look at the brushed up crescents on
rushing rivers and salmon leaping

to the levels of their birth

Molecules twinkle like stars
and stars sigh from

ecstasy as they

blend back into day

7/18

TRY TO DESCRIBE LIGHT

Try to describe light
and it's hopeless

Nothing can quite catch in words
luminous nothingness

Hold something up in light
and it's revealed in it say a

miniature Easter Island head
now brought out in its

full strangeness by the
surrounding illumination

But how can you hold up something like
light in light and hope to achieve

the thing the flash the flat surrounding
splashy airiness of brightness

in whose beneficence everything including
us is revealed?

And this is just physical light
not that which is followed

cavern within cavern within
a numinous blue

and in a dimension that makes this
dimension we're in with all its

tornadoes seem slim and
overly rambunctious

The whinny of a horse
echoes down the centuries

Here's Genghis Khan on one
a black outline against blare

light of the steppes then the
flickering red light of whole

cities being burnt to the ground

And the uncanny and indescribable
light of Ibn 'Arabi's inner

world of whole strange neon
coral reefs of spiritual realities

he's described in such minute detail and
literary magnificence between the

pages of either unopened or un-
comprehended oceans of high

reverberant light

And that's only a
tiny fraction

(Door opens —
light floods the room)

(Door closes —
blackness)

7/22

OKAY THE COCKSCOMB OF THE ROOSTER

for Omar Benhalim

Okay the cockscomb of the rooster and the
boot heel of the Nazi do they

both have light?

The orchard of mustard flowers and the
landing of the Conquistadores in

Mexico as well as the silver setting of
the Queen of Norway at tea and the

forced cannibalism atop the Alps by the
Argentine soccer team —

*Do they all evince vast innermost
illumination of one degree or*

another?

The mouse sniffing its way forward behind my
plasterboard walls in the dark and

a pair of eagles wheeling in a
white sky as well as

a decision deep in consultation by the
President of the United States behind

drawn presidential drapes and
fresh water dolphins deep in

murky Amazon water with their
very long proboscises —

all equally aglitter? All emitting
elemental divine wattage at

varying intensities?
Can I even finish this poem in a

considerable flourish of lit wisdom or at
least glimmering appreciation and

spotlit gratitude for the slightest sliver of
light the most inconsiderable of

incandescences at the far
margins of all things

or in point of fact
at their

absolute centers?

7/25

HAVING LEFT THE FUNERAL

Having left the funeral before
anyone was dead

I came upon a waterless ocean
and drank my thirst

Everyone's so filled with wonder

Luminous squares begin circulating in
the most out-of-the-way places and most

intimate spaces

If God walked in right now
all the universes His overcoat

no one would be surprised
though I am that I could even

say such a thing
but that's how things are when

the sky underfoot begins singing
and the earth above smiles to hear such

crazed but
beneficent music

7/26

WATER

What is this water God's created for us
the blood of angels

that circulates through the air
and lays down in cupped crevices?

Rolls down hills into huge oceanic basins and
falls as direct mercy from the skies

onto our tin roofs like Trinidadian steel drums
and into our upraised mouths to

slake thirsts way down into our
bodies and blood so brother and

sister to genderless water itself
who goes on and on in rivers and

bloodstreams with Mona Lisa serenity
when it isn't rampaging with mastodon

majesty in floods and maelstroms

Dear unbelievable water I just
drank from my flask not even

realizing how thirsty I was in this
heat wondering what the wonderful watery

miracle it is

transparent in its humble straightforwardness
supple in its gravitational submissiveness

so smooth and innocuous yet capable of
cutting canyons out of obdurate rock

A force to contend with when it comes in
giant tsunami-size wrecking

tourist hotels and putting fishing boats in
trees

But what a gulp that lit me into
serenity suddenly!

This mystery element without which
we'd be parched and rusty Martians

for all eternity!

7/31

MIXED METAPHORS

1

Slowly the body becomes like a
Swiss cheese with round areas of emptiness

where a wind blows through the
openings that's traveled the

length of our lives but comes from
a divine peak that saw us

be born and is
always with us

within us

But what a wind! Howl of
Krakatoa tremendousness that

occasionally shakes its mane through us
like a prize thoroughbred certain of its

pedigree

out to the extents of our
fingers and toes and our

other extremities until we are
stretched webs of light the wind can

batter like sails on the
high seas

2

"Mixed metaphors are my business"
said life itself to itself as it

stood by itself
on the boulevard of dreams

"Can't live with 'em can't
live without 'em — why

take the rain coming down like
cats and dogs for example

or like a cat running across the
piano keys until the

stuck car horn of its thunderclap
wakes us from dryness to a

flash flood of memories and drip-sized
global hints of the future"

8/5

THE SHEER AUDACITY

Given the sheer audacity of our continuation
supported at all moments and at all

physical and metaphysical points by
God's continual Generosity alone

So that even immobile or sitting almost
stiffly we're actually bodies suspended

in silken webs of purest light spun fine
yet to outward physical eyes look as if we're

going about our days and stretched
out by night in normal physical fashion

with whole herds of
imaginary animals moving below us

We say this and that we
do this and that but given the

sheer bravado of our rising and engaging with
even the most innocuous of objects or

situations here at this end point of
millennia of human development that we can

look back down its long corridor by
squinting slightly and there see

figures emitting as well as surrounded by
constant as well as

inconstant incandescence as they

swim upright through the air
entering each space that is in fact

their very selves they fold into

Adams and Eves of intensest illumination!

But given our sheer bravado and audacity
and that the insides of us are inhabited quite

realistically by the living history of saints of both
sexes and all races by which I mean

gorgeously and splendidly awake beings in
action or at rest in society or

momentarily isolated in desert wastes or
mountain caves melting the ice around them

by the intensities of their unbewildered or
vastly bewildered hearts' fiery hibiscus flowerings

Given all this
that we in our encrusted individualities

would say between each word and between each

breath the grateful praise that
links us indissolubly to our constantly

incandescent origin whose blinding radiance
outlines in halo the most

inconsequential spider and most
spatially momentary gnat

whose tiny head like a great horse
rears up through the sky

its silent whinny filling all heaven

8/11

WRAPPED AROUND THE COSMOS

There's the man who climbed a tall ladder
until the rungs disappeared

but he kept on climbing

Or the man who spread his arms to fly
and he didn't so much rise in the air

as the earth below him fell away
and he remained suspended

Or the woman who danced so fast she
lost her outlines altogether and

vanished in a puff of rose-scented smoke

All these hyper-phenomena taking place right in
our own backyard on earth with its

vistas of star-lined and diamond-studded
galaxies whizzing by around us

and each of these three with those
constellational smiles on their faces

moonlit at the edges and sunlit at their
centers in the deep heart's core

Each vibrational reality rooted in

mysteries to us but natural to God

Who at His behest has made this
miraculous landscaped and cloud-capped

towering earth with its lizards and lions prowling
freely and blinking their

beautiful eyes on worlds we can
only imagine

And the ladder-climbing man climbed up out of
this one into a completely new one whose

materiality was made up of various tones of a
crystalline and sibilant sound beyond our usual hearing

And the suspended gentleman while in that state
found himself solving impossible mathematical formulas and

proving outlandish hypotheses of physics

And the woman as well grew accustomed to living
bodiless until it seemed it was

we who were smoke and rosiness
wisping away at last into nothingness

while she was God's intimate sweetheart
wrapped around the cosmos like a cloud

8/13

INDEX OF TITLES

ABOUT THE AUTHOR

Born in 1940 in Oakland, California, Daniel Abdal-Hayy Moore's first book of poems, *Dawn Visions*, was published by Lawrence Ferlinghetti of City Lights Books, San Francisco, in 1964, and the second in 1972, *Burnt Heart/Ode to the War Dead*. He created and directed *The Floating Lotus Magic Opera Company* in Berkeley, California in the late 60s, and presented two major productions, *The Walls Are Running Blood*, and *Bliss Apocalypse*. He became a Sufi Muslim in 1970, performed the Hajj in 1972, and lived and traveled throughout Morocco, Spain, Algeria and Nigeria, landing in California and publishing *The Desert is the Only Way Out*, and *Chronicles of Akhira* in the early 80s (Zilzal Press). Residing in Philadelphia since 1990, in 1996 he published *The Ramadan Sonnets* (Jusoor/City Lights), and in 2002, *The Blind Beekeeper* (Jusoor/Syracuse University Press). He has been the major editor for a number of works, including *The Burdah* of Shaykh Busiri, translated by Shaykh Hamza Yusuf, and the poetry of Palestinian poet, Mahmoud Darwish, translated by Munir Akash. He is also widely published on the worldwide web: *The American Muslim*, *DeenPort*, and his own website and poetry blog, among others: www. danielmoorepoetry.com, www.ecstaticxchange.wordpress.com. He has been poetry editor for *Islamica Magazine*, and *Seasons Journal*, a new translation by Munir Akash of *State of Siege*, by Mahmoud Darwish, from Syracuse University Press, and *The Prayer of the Oppressed* of Imam Nasir al-Dar'i, translated by Hamza Yusuf. The Ecstatic Exchange Series is bringing out the extensive body of his works of poetry (a complete list of published works on page 2).

POETIC WORKS by Daniel Abdal-Hayy Moore
Published and Unpublished

Dawn Visions (published by City Lights, 1964)
Burnt Heart/Ode to the War Dead (published by City Lights, 1972)
This Body of Black Light Gone Through the Diamond (printed by Fred Stone, Cambridge, Mass, 1965)
On The Streets at Night Alone (1965?)
All Hail the Surgical Lamp (1967)
States of Amazement (1970)

Abdallah Jones and the Disappearing-Dust Caper (published by The Ecstatic Exchange/Crescent Series, 2006)
'Ala ud-Deen and the Magic Lamp
The Chronicles of Akhira (1981) (published by Zilzal Press with Typoglyphs by Karl Kempton, 1986)(published in Sparrow on the Prophet's Tomb by The Ecstatic Exchange, 2009)
Mouloud (1984) (A Zilzal Press chapbook, 1995)(published in Sparrow on the Prophet's Tomb by The Ecstatic Exchange, 2009)
Man is the Crown of Creation (1984)
The Look of the Lion (The Parabolas of Sight) (1984)
The Desert is the Only Way Out (completed 4/21/84) (Zilzal Press chapbook, 1985)
Atomic Dance (1984) (am here books, 1988)
Outlandish Tales (1984)
Awake as Never Before (12/26/84) (Zilzal Press chapbook, 1993)
Glorious Intervals (1/1/85) (Zilzal Press chapbook, ?)
Long Days on Earth/Book I (1/28 – 8/30/85)
Long Days on Earth/Book II (Hayy Ibn Yaqzan)
Long Days on Earth/Book III (1/22/86)
Long Days on Earth/Book IV (1986)
The Ramadan Sonnets (Long Days on Earth/Book V) (5/9 – 6/11/86) (published by Jusoor/City Lights Books, 1996) (republished as Ramadan Sonnets by The Ecstatic Exchange, 2005)
Long Days on Earth/Book VI (6-8/30/86)
Holograms (9/4/86 – 3/26/87)
History of the World (The Epic of Man's Survival) (4/7 – 6/18/87)

Exploratory Odes (6/25 – 10/18/87)

The Man at the End of the World (11/11 – 12/10/87)

The Perfect Orchestra (3/30 – 7/25/88) (published by The Ecstatic Exchange, 2009)

Fed from Underground Springs (7/30 – 11/23/88)

Ideas of the Heart (11/27/88 – 5/5/89)

New Poems (scattered poems, out of series, from 3/24 – 8/9/89)

Facing Mecca (5/16 – 11/11/89)

A Maddening Disregard for the Passage of Time (11/17/89 – 5/20/90) (published by The Ecstatic Exchange, 2009)

The Heart Falls in Love with Visions of Perfection (6/15/90 – 6/2/91)

Like When You Wave at a Train and the Train Hoots Back at You (Farid's Book) (6/11 – 7/26/91) (published by The Ecstatic Exchange, 2008)

Orpheus Meets Morpheus (8/1/91– 3/14/92)

The Puzzle (3/21/92 – 8/17/93)

The Greater Vehicle (10/17/93 – 4/30/94)

A Hundred Little 3-D Pictures (5/14/94 – 9/11/95)

The Angel Broadcast (9/29 – 12/17/95)

Mecca/Medina Time-Warp (12/19/95 – 1/6/96) (published as a Zilzal Press chapbook, 1996)(published in Sparrow on the Prophet's Tomb by The Ecstatic Exchange, 2009)

Miracle Songs for the Millennium (1/20 – 10/16/96)

The Blind Beekeeper (11/15/96 – 5/30/97) (published 2002 by Jusoor/ Syracuse University Press)

Chants for the Beauty Feast (6/3 – 10/28/97)(published by The Ecstatic Exchange, 2011)

You Open a Door and it's a Starry Night (10/29/97 – 5/23/98) (published by The Ecstatic Exchange, 2009)

Salt Prayers (5/29 – 10/24/98) (published by The Ecstatic Exchange, 2005)

Some (10/25/98 – 4/25/99)

Flight to Egypt (5/1 – 5/16/99)

I Imagine a Lion (5/21 – 11/15/99) (published by The Ecstatic Exchange, 2006)

Millennial Prognostications (11/25/99 – 2/2/2000) (published by the Ecstatic Exchange, 2009)

Shaking the Quicksilver Pool (2/4 – 10/8/2000) (published by The Ecstatic Exchange, 2009)

Blood Songs (10/9/2000 – 4/3/2001)

The Music Space (4/10 – 9/16/2001) (published by The Ecstatic Exchange, 2007)

Where Death Goes (9/20/2001 – 5/1/2002) (published by The Ecstatic Exchange, 2009)

The Flame of Transformation Turns to Light (99 Ghazals Written in English) (5/14 – 8/21/2002) (published by The Ecstatic Exchange, 2007)

Through Rose-Colored Glasses (7/22/2002 – 1/15/2003) (published by The Ecstatic Exchange, 2007)

Psalms for the Broken-Hearted (1/22 – 5/25/2003) (published by The Ecstatic Exchange, 2006)

Hoopoe's Argument (5/27 – 9/18/03)

Love is a Letter Burning in a High Wind (9/21 – 11/6/2003) (published by The Ecstatic Exchange, 2006)

Laughing Buddha/Weeping Sufi (11/7/2003 – 1/10/2004) (published by The Ecstatic Exchange, 2005)

Mars and Beyond (1/20 – 3/29/2004) (published by The Ecstatic Exchange, 2005)

Underwater Galaxies (4/5 – 7/21/2004) (published by The Ecstatic Exchange, 2007)

Cooked Oranges (7/23/2004 – 1/24/2005 (published by The Ecstatic Exchange, 2007)

Holiday from the Perfect Crime (1/25 – 6/11/2005)

Stories Too Fiery to Sing Too Watery to Whisper (6/13 – 10/24/2005)

Coattails of the Saint (10/26/2005 – 5/10/2006) (published by The Ecstatic Exchange, 2006)

In the Realm of Neither (5/14 – 11/12/06) (published by The Ecstatic Exchange, 2008)

Invention of the Wheel (11/13/06 – 6/10/07) (published by The Ecstatic Exchange, 2010)

The Sound of Geese Over the House (6/15 – 11/4/07)

The Fire Eater's Lunchbreak (11/11/07 – 5/19/2008) (published by The Ecstatic Exchange, 2008)

Sparks Off the Main Strike (5/24/2008 – 1/10/2009) (published by The Ecstatic Excange, 2010)

Stretched Out on Amethysts (1/13 – 9/17/2009) (published by The Ecstatic Exchange, 2010)

The Throne Perpendicular to All that is Horizontal (9/18/09 – 1/25/10)

In Constant Incandescence (2/10 – 8/13/10) (published by The Ecstatic Exchange, 2011

The Caged Bear Spies the Angel (8/30/10 –)

LU0005372576 0